THE SECRET SCIENCE OF HOW TO SELL

How to turn words, into wealth

Chris Edun

Table of Contents

INTRODUCTION

Welcome to the dynamic world of sales, where persuasion meets strategy, and success is forged through the art of communication.

The world of sales is where charisma equals commission, and rejection is just another step towards that elusive yes. Brace yourself for a rollercoaster ride of persuasion, where your product knowledge becomes your superpower, and rejection is merely a friendly tap on the shoulder saying, "Try again, champ!" Welcome to the school of sales, where closing deals is an art, and your pitch is the masterpiece in progress. Get ready to charm your way to quotas, because in this classroom, the only thing higher than your targets is your confidence.

I have condensed over 15 years of personal sales experience, from selling double glazing to the working class, all the way to managing multi-million pound portfolios for HNW's. In the toughest corporate racket, which is hard sales I can finally say i made it. On my journey to success I attended multiple sales seminars, private training,even once with the infamous Jordan Belfort.

Regardless of what you think of him, the guy is a sales guru and really understands what makes people buy. I've also read hundreds of sales books,most lacking key fundamentals with real world examples of how to get the job done.

If you read, memorize and study the gems of knowledge in this book. You will unleash a power within you and manifest real world tangible success.

Do not rush the process.

Repetition is the mother of learning.

Read this book at least three times. I have made this sales manual as concise as possible to make this more feasible.

I have cut the fat from the beef and left you with a lean prime cut.

All you need to do is season and cook but make sure you dont over do it, unless you want to burn the meal.

This is a key fundamental in sales, sell the sizzle not the bacon.

In this comprehensive guide, we will navigate the intricacies of modern selling, uncovering proven techniques, and empowering you with the skills to not just meet, but exceed your sales goals. Get ready to elevate your approach, master the psychology of selling, and unlock the keys to building lasting, fruitful relationships with your clients. Whether you're a seasoned sales professional or just starting your journey, this book is your roadmap to unparalleled success in the ever-evolving landscape of sales. Lets begin.

LESSON 1: THE GENESIS OF SALES

In the annals of human history, the concept of sales finds its roots in the age-old practice of bartering. Early civilizations engaged in the exchange of goods and services, laying the groundwork for the fundamental principles of sales we recognize today.

As societies evolved, so did the methods of trade. Ancient marketplaces became bustling hubs where merchants showcased their wares, employing persuasive techniques to attract potential buyers. The birth of currency further fueled the growth of sales, transforming transactions into a more fluid and standardized process.

The Silk Road and Beyond

The Silk Road, a historic network of trade routes connecting East and West, played a pivotal role in the development of sales. Merchants traversed vast distances, facilitating the exchange of goods, cultures, and ideas. This intricate web of commerce not only enhanced the art of negotiation but also introduced diverse sales tactics shaped by the rich tapestry of cultures along the route.

The Renaissance and the Art of Persuasion

During the Renaissance, a shift occurred in the perception of salesmanship. The emergence of a burgeoning middle class created new opportunities, and individuals sought to distinguish themselves through refined selling skills. The notion of persuasion became an art form, with thinkers like Machiavelli offering insights into the psychology of influence. The merchant class flourished, contributing to the evolution of sales as a strategic endeavor.

The Industrial Revolution and Mass Marketing

The advent of the Industrial Revolution marked a paradigm shift in sales. Mass production led to increased competition, necessitating more sophisticated sales approaches. The rise of department stores and mail-order catalogs ushered in a new era of mass marketing, where businesses embraced advertising and promotional campaigns to reach wider audiences.

The 20th Century and Professional Salesmanship

The 20th century witnessed the formalization of sales as a profession. Sales training programs emerged, emphasizing the importance of product knowledge, communication skills, and customer relationships. The introduction of door-to-door sales, telemarketing, and eventually e-commerce further diversified the sales landscape.

The Digital Age and Data-Driven Sales

The 21st century brought about a revolution in sales with the advent of the internet. E-commerce platforms, social media, and big data analytics transformed the way products were marketed and sold. Personalization became key as businesses leveraged data insights to tailor their offerings to individual preferences.

The Future of Sales

As we stand on the cusp of a new era, the future of sales promises continued innovation. Artificial intelligence, virtual reality, and advanced analytics are poised to reshape the sales landscape once again. However, amidst the technological advancements, the core principles of understanding customer needs and building lasting relationships remain the bedrock of successful salesmanship.

LESSON 2 : THE ART OF EXCHANGE

In a time before time, echoes of ancient wisdom resonate through the marketplaces of antiquity, where the art of sales took its humble roots. Wise men and traders alike left behind words that transcended eras, capturing the essence of commerce. Let us venture into the past and unveil the timeless quotes that echo the spirit of salesmanship.

*** Confucius on Integrity in Trade ***

"In trade, as in life, let your integrity shine brighter than the gold you seek to exchange."

Confucius, the ancient Chinese philosopher, emphasized the importance of honesty and integrity in all human interactions, including the intricate dance of buying and selling. His words echo through the bustling markets where trust was the currency that forged enduring connections.

*** Aristotle's Insight on Persuasion ***

"The art of persuasion lies not in the words spoken, but in understanding the needs of others and fulfilling them."

Aristotle, the Greek philosopher, recognized the subtle dance of persuasion as a key element in the sales realm. His words illuminate the path for those seeking not just transactions but lasting partnerships, founded on a deep understanding of the buyer's desires.

*** The Silk Road Traders' Proverb ***

"A fair deal is a bridge built of mutual respect, connecting distant lands with threads of trust."

Along the ancient Silk Road, where goods traversed continents, traders shared a proverb emphasizing the enduring nature of fair deals. This sentiment reflects the interconnectedness of distant cultures and the foundational role of trust in fostering prosperous trade routes.

*** Roman Stoicism on Adversity ***

"In the face of challenges, the resilient trader finds opportunity, turning adversity into the coinage of success."

Stoic philosophers in ancient Rome recognized the inevitability of challenges in business. Their wisdom guides the salesperson to embrace difficulties as stepping stones toward greater achievement, forging resilience in the crucible of commerce.

*** Indian Merchant's Reflection on Customer Satisfaction ***

"A satisfied customer is a jewel in the merchant's treasury, for their contentment multiplies through word of mouth like the ripples of a serene pond."

In the ancient markets of India, merchants valued the satisfaction of their customers as a precious asset. This timeless insight underscores the enduring power of positive customer experiences in building a thriving trade.

As we traverse the ancient corridors of commerce, these quotes stand as pillars, guiding the salesperson through the labyrinth of human transactions. In each word, a nugget of wisdom beckons, reminding us that the art of sales transcends time, echoing through the ages in the eternal dance of give and take.

LESSON 3: IGNITING SALES VISION AND AMBITION

To maneuvre in the sales world, a compelling vision and unwavering ambition can be the catalyst for unparalleled success. As sales professionals embark on their journey, they must cultivate a clear vision that transcends quotas and transactions, reaching towards the horizon of long-term impact.

*** Setting the Stage ***

A visionary salesperson doesn't merely focus on meeting targets but envisions the transformative power their product or service holds for customers. This vision becomes a guiding light, propelling them beyond the mundane and infusing their sales approach with purpose. It's about understanding the profound impact their offerings can have on individuals, businesses, and industries.

*** Beyond Quotas ***

Ambition in sales extends beyond the attainment of quarterly goals. It involves a hunger for continuous improvement, a thirst for knowledge about the market, and an unyielding desire to surpass one's own limits. Ambitious sales professionals view challenges not as obstacles but as stepping stones to greater heights, pushing themselves to elevate their skills and refine their strategies.

* Crafting a Visionary Narrative *

A sales vision, akin to a compelling story, captivates both the storyteller and the audience. Successful salespeople are adept at weaving a narrative that goes beyond product features and pricing. They articulate a future where their offerings become indispensable, painting a picture of value that resonates with clients and stakeholders alike.

* Resilience in the Face of Rejection *

In the pursuit of ambitious sales goals, rejection becomes an inevitable companion. Visionary sales professionals don't see rejection as failure but as feedback, an opportunity to refine their approach. Ambition fuels resilience, enabling them to bounce back stronger, armed with insights and a determination to convert setbacks into stepping stones.

* Collaboration and Mentorship *

A vision is nurtured not in isolation but through collaboration. Ambitious salespeople seek out mentorship, leveraging the experience of seasoned professionals to refine their vision and enhance their skills. This collaborative spirit fosters a culture of continuous learning, where the ambitious strive to absorb insights from both successes and failures.

* Adapting to Market Dynamics *

A rigid vision can become a liability in the dynamic landscape of sales. Ambitious professionals remain adaptable, embracing change as an opportunity rather than a threat. They constantly reassess their vision in light of market shifts, ensuring it remains aligned with evolving customer needs and industry trends.

In the realm of sales, vision and ambition are the twin engines that propel individuals toward unprecedented success. A clear vision provides direction, while ambition fuels the relentless pursuit of excellence. As sales professionals cultivate these qualities, they not only exceed targets but also leave an indelible mark on the ever-evolving canvas of the sales landscape.

LESSON 4: IGNITING PERSONAL MOTIVATION

In the vast landscape of self-discovery, personal motivation emerges as a guiding force, propelling individuals toward their aspirations. Understanding and cultivating this inner drive is akin to unlocking a wellspring of potential.

*** Discovering Passion ***

Motivation often finds its roots in passion. Identify the activities that ignite a spark within you. What makes your heart race and your mind buzz with excitement? Embrace these passions as they hold the key to sustained motivation.

*** Setting Meaningful Goals ***

Define clear and achievable goals that align with your values. Break them into smaller milestones, providing a roadmap for progress. This structured approach not only fuels motivation but also offers a tangible sense of accomplishment.

*** Overcoming Challenges ***

Obstacles are inevitable, yet they serve as catalysts for personal growth. View challenges not as roadblocks, but as opportunities to refine your character and resilience. Embrace the journey, for it is through overcoming adversity that motivation is fortified.

* Cultivating Discipline *

Motivation often wanes, but discipline acts as a steadfast companion. Establish daily habits that align with your goals. Consistency in small actions creates a ripple effect, reinforcing your commitment and fanning the flames of motivation.

* Positive Self-Talk *

Your inner dialogue shapes your reality. Replace self-doubt with affirmations and constructive thoughts. Encourage yourself in times of difficulty, recognizing that setbacks are temporary and part of the journey towards personal growth.

* Surrounding Yourself with Positivity *

Your environment plays a crucial role in sustaining motivation. Engage with individuals who uplift and inspire. Create a supportive network that fosters an atmosphere of encouragement, as collective motivation can be a powerful force.

* Celebrating Progress *

Acknowledge and celebrate your achievements, no matter how small. This reinforces the connection between effort and success, reinforcing the belief that your actions yield tangible results. Celebration becomes a source of renewed motivation.

* Adapting to Change *

Flexibility is key on the path to personal motivation. Embrace change as an opportunity for growth, adapting your goals and strategies accordingly. A dynamic approach ensures that motivation persists despite life's unpredictable nature.

In the intricate dance of personal motivation, each step forward builds momentum. Nurture your passions, set meaningful goals, and persevere through challenges. As you cultivate discipline, maintain positive self-talk, and foster a supportive environment, you'll find motivation not as a fleeting emotion but as an enduring force propelling you towards your aspirations.

LESSON 5: POWER LESSONS FROM LES BROWN

In the realm of motivational speaking, Les Brown stands as a beacon of inspiration. His words have the power to ignite passion, unlock potential, and propel individuals towards greatness. This chapter delves into ten profound quotes from Les Brown, each carrying a valuable lesson for those on the journey of personal development.

1:"Shoot for the moon. Even if you miss, you'll land among the stars."

Les Brown encourages us to dream big, to set audacious goals that stretch our limits. Embrace the pursuit of lofty aspirations, for in the effort to reach them, we discover untapped potential and unforeseen opportunities.

2:"Your level of belief in yourself will inevitably manifest itself in whatever you do."

Belief is the driving force behind success. Les Brown emphasizes the importance of cultivating self-confidence and unwavering belief in one's abilities. The stronger your belief, the greater your capacity to overcome obstacles and achieve your goals.

3:"You don't have to be great to get started, but you have to get started to be great."

Procrastination is the enemy of progress. Les Brown encourages action, emphasizing that the journey towards greatness begins with the first step. Don't wait for perfection; start where you are, and greatness will follow.

4: "Too many of us are not living our dreams because we are living our fears."

Fear has the power to paralyze dreams and stifle potential. Les Brown challenges us to confront our fears head-on, to break free from the chains that hold us back, and to pursue our dreams with unwavering determination.

5:"Life has no limitations, except the ones you make."

Les Brown reminds us that our potential is boundless, constrained only by the limitations we impose on ourselves. Break free from self-imposed barriers, embrace possibilities, and unleash the full extent of your capabilities.

6:"If you set goals and go after them with all the determination you can muster, your gifts will take you places that will amaze you."

Goals provide direction, and determination fuels progress. Les Brown emphasizes the transformative power of setting clear goals and pursuing them relentlessly, unlocking hidden talents and propelling individuals to unexpected heights.

7: "You are never too old to set another goal or to dream a new

dream."

Age should never be a barrier to personal growth and reinvention. Les Brown encourages us to continuously set new goals, dream new dreams, and approach each day with a sense of wonder and possibility, regardless of our age.

8:*"It's not over until I win."*

A mantra of resilience and determination, this quote reflects Les Brown's unwavering commitment to success. Embrace a mindset that refuses to accept defeat, understanding that setbacks are temporary, and victory is inevitable with persistence.

9: *"You must be willing to do the things today others won't do, in order to have the things tomorrow others won't have."*

Success often requires unconventional efforts and a willingness to go beyond the ordinary. Les Brown challenges us to embrace the discomfort of hard work and dedication, knowing that the rewards will be extraordinary.

10. *"It's not where you start, it's how you finish."*

Les Brown's words encapsulate the essence of resilience and perseverance. Regardless of the challenges faced at the beginning, focus on finishing strong. Your journey may be tough, but the ending is within your control.

Les Brown's wisdom continues to resonate, urging us to live a life filled with purpose, determination, and unwavering self-belief. Let these quotes serve as a guiding light on your journey towards personal and professional fulfillment.

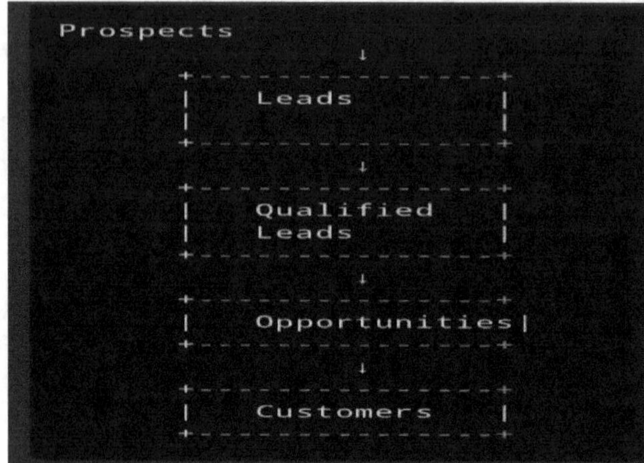

Fig 1. A simplified Sales Funnel

LESSON 6: THE ZEN OF SELLING

In sales, a harmonious convergence with New Age philosophy can bring forth a transformative approach. Embracing the principles of mindfulness, empathy, and interconnectedness can elevate the art of selling beyond transactional exchanges. Here, we explore how New Age philosophy intertwines with the dynamics of sales, creating a synergy that transcends traditional paradigms.

Mindful Selling

In the hustle of the sales world, mindfulness becomes a guiding force. Practicing presence and awareness allows sales professionals to connect authentically with clients. The concept of being in the moment encourages active listening, enabling sellers to understand the unique needs and desires of their customers. By immersing themselves fully in the sales conversation, practitioners of mindful selling foster genuine relationships and build trust.

Empathy in Action

New Age philosophy places a profound emphasis on empathy – the ability to understand and share the feelings of others. In sales, empathy becomes a potent tool for deciphering the emotional landscape of potential clients. Sellers attuned to the needs and concerns of their customers can tailor their approach, creating a personalized experience that resonates on a deeper level. This empathic connection not only facilitates smoother transactions but also engenders lasting client relationships.

The Law of Attraction in Sales

In the world of New Age thinking, the Law of Attraction asserts that positive or negative thoughts bring positive or negative experiences into a person's life. Applying this principle to sales, sellers can cultivate a positive mindset that attracts success. Visualizing success, setting affirmations, and maintaining a constructive outlook contribute to a magnetic energy that draws opportunities and favorable outcomes.

Interconnected Commerce

New Age philosophy recognizes the interconnectedness of all things. In sales, this interconnectedness manifests in the acknowledgment that every transaction has ripple effects. By fostering a sense of responsibility and ethical behavior, sales professionals contribute to a positive business ecosystem. Sustainable and socially responsible practices not only align with New Age values but also resonate with an increasingly conscious consumer base.

Mind-Body-Soul Selling

The holistic approach of New Age philosophy extends to the concept of mind-body-soul selling. Beyond the transactional aspect, sales become a transformative experience for both the seller and the buyer. Sellers who align their values with the products or services they represent infuse a sense of purpose into their work. This purpose-driven approach creates a resonance that goes beyond immediate gains, fostering a sense of fulfillment and satisfaction.

In conclusion, the marriage of New Age philosophy and sales offers a holistic and mindful approach to the art of selling. By incorporating principles of mindfulness, empathy, the Law of Attraction, and recognizing the interconnected nature of commerce, sales professionals can elevate their practice to a higher plane. The result is not just successful transactions but the creation of meaningful and lasting connections in the ever-evolving landscape of sales.

LESSON 7: VISUALIZATION AND AFFIRMATIONS

Now that you've set your intentions and clarified your goals using the law of attraction, it's time to delve into the power of visualization and affirmations. These practices are instrumental in aligning your thoughts and feelings with the reality you wish to manifest.

STEP 1: CREATE A QUIET SPACE

Find a comfortable and quiet space where you won't be interrupted. This could be a corner in your room, a cozy chair, or even a peaceful outdoor spot. The key is to minimize distractions and create an environment conducive to focused thinking.

STEP 2: RELAXATION TECHNIQUES

Begin with deep breaths to calm your mind and body. Consider incorporating relaxation techniques such as meditation or progressive muscle relaxation to enhance your focus and reduce stress. The more relaxed you are, the more receptive you become to positive thoughts.

STEP 3: VISUALIZATION

Close your eyes and vividly picture your desired outcome. Imagine every detail, from the sights and sounds to the emotions you would experience. Make the scenario as real and detailed as possible. Engage your senses and immerse yourself in the experience as if it's happening right now.

STEP 4: POSITIVE AFFIRMATIONS

Craft positive affirmations that resonate with your goals. These statements should be present tense, as if you've already achieved what you desire. Repeat these affirmations aloud or in your mind. For example, if your goal is financial abundance, affirmations like "I am attracting wealth into my life effortlessly" can reinforce positive beliefs.

STEP 5: EMOTIONAL CONNECTION

As you visualize and repeat affirmations, focus on the positive emotions associated with your goals. Feel the joy, gratitude, and fulfillment as if you've already manifested your desires. Emotions are a powerful magnet for attracting what you want.

STEP 6: CONSISTENCY IS KEY

Consistency is crucial in the practice of visualization and affirmations. Set aside time each day to engage in these exercises. Over time, this repetition strengthens the neural pathways associated with your goals, making it easier for your mind to accept them as reality.

STEP 7: EXPRESS GRATITUDE

Express gratitude for the manifestations that are on their way. Gratitude reinforces positive energy and signals to the universe that you appreciate the abundance that is coming into your life.

Remember, the law of attraction works through the alignment of thoughts, feelings, and actions. Visualization and affirmations act as tools to reshape your mindset and attract the experiences you desire. Stay committed, maintain a positive outlook, and watch as your intentions begin to materialize.

LESSON 8: MASTERING TELESALES

Mastering the art of telesales is essential for success. This chapter delves into the key fundamentals that form the backbone of effective telesales strategies.

Building Rapport over the Phone

Establishing a connection with potential customers is the first step to success. Telesales professionals must hone their communication skills, employing a friendly and engaging tone to build trust and rapport from the first "Hello."

Product Knowledge Mastery

A deep understanding of the product or service being offered is paramount. Telesales reps should be well-versed in the features, benefits, and unique selling points, enabling them to articulate value propositions convincingly.

Effective Communication Skills

Clear and concise communication is the heartbeat of telesales. Reps must convey information persuasively, adapting their language and pitch to the customer's needs and preferences.

Active Listening Techniques

Telesales is a two-way street. Cultivating active listening skills allows reps to grasp customer concerns, tailor their responses, and demonstrate genuine interest in addressing the client's needs.

Overcoming Objections

Every sales call presents challenges. Successful telesales professionals are adept at identifying and overcoming objections by turning them into opportunities. This requires a combination of empathy, confidence, and well-prepared responses.

Time Management and Goal Setting

Telesales is a numbers game, and effective time management is crucial. Reps should set realistic goals, prioritize leads, and allocate time strategically to maximize productivity.

CRM Utilization

Customer Relationship Management (CRM) tools are indispensable in telesales. Mastery of CRM systems enables reps to track interactions, personalize communication, and stay organized in managing leads and opportunities.

Continuous Training and Adaptation

The telesales landscape is ever-evolving. A commitment to ongoing training keeps reps updated on industry trends, new products, and effective sales techniques. Adaptability is a key trait in staying ahead in this dynamic field.

Ethical Practices and Compliance

Maintaining integrity is non-negotiable. Telesales professionals must adhere to ethical practices, respecting customer privacy and complying with relevant regulations to build a trustworthy reputation.

Resilience and Positive Mindset

Telesales can be challenging, with rejection being a constant companion. Building resilience and maintaining a positive mindset are essential for navigating the ups and downs of the profession, ensuring long-term success.

As we explore the depths of telesales, remember that mastering these fundamentals is a continuous journey. The following chapters will delve deeper into each aspect, providing practical tips and real-world examples to guide you toward becoming a telesales maestro.

LESSON 9: MASTERING THE ART OF COLD CALLING

Cold calling can be a powerful tool for reaching potential clients and expanding your business. Here's a step-by-step guide to help you navigate the nuances of this essential skill.

1. Research Your Prospect:

Before dialing, gather information about the company and individual you're calling. Understanding their needs and challenges will make your conversation more relevant and engaging.

2. Craft a Compelling Opening:

Start with a concise and attention-grabbing introduction. Clearly state who you are, your company, and the purpose of your call. Make it about them by highlighting a common pain point or challenge.

3. Be Confident and Enthusiastic:

Confidence is key. Speak clearly and with enthusiasm to convey your passion for your product or service. A positive tone can make a significant impact on the prospect's perception.

4. Keep it Concise:

Respect your prospect's time by keeping your pitch concise. Clearly articulate the value proposition and how your solution can address their specific needs. Aim for a pitch that takes no more than 30 seconds.

5. Listen Actively:

Once you've presented your pitch, listen attentively to the prospect's response. Understand their concerns and interests, and tailor your conversation accordingly. This demonstrates your commitment to meeting their needs.

6. Overcome Objections Gracefully:

Anticipate common objections and prepare responses that address them confidently. Acknowledge concerns and pivot the conversation back to the benefits and solutions your product or service offers.

7. Personalize Your Approach:

Every prospect is unique. Tailor your communication style to match theirs and adjust your pitch based on their industry or specific challenges. Personalization can build a stronger connection.

8. Set Clear Next Steps:

End the call by defining clear next steps. Whether it's scheduling a follow-up meeting, sending additional information, or arranging a product demonstration, ensure both parties know what to expect.

9. Follow Up Promptly:

After the call, send a personalized follow-up email expressing gratitude for their time. Reinforce key points from the conversation and provide any promised information promptly.

10. Continuously Learn and Adapt:

Cold calling is an evolving skill. Analyze your calls, identify what works well, and continuously refine your approach. Stay informed about industry trends and adjust your strategy accordingly.

Mastering the art of cold calling takes practice and persistence. By refining your techniques, adapting to feedback, and maintaining a positive mindset, you'll increase your chances of turning cold calls into valuable business opportunities.

LESSON 10: NURTURING CONNECTIONS THROUGH WARM CALLING

While cold calling is an effective strategy, warm calling takes relationship-building to the next level. Establishing a warm connection with a prospect involves leveraging existing relationships and prior interactions. Here's a guide to mastering the art of warm calling:

1. Leverage Existing Connections:

Begin by identifying mutual connections or shared experiences. Whether it's a colleague, a common industry event, or a referral, mentioning these connections in your opening can create an instant sense of familiarity.

2. Reference Previous Interactions:

If you've had prior engagements with the prospect, refer to those interactions. Acknowledge any meetings, emails, or events you both attended. This not only refreshes their memory but also shows your commitment to the relationship.

3. Personalize Your Outreach:

Tailor your message to the prospect's specific needs and interests. Reference details from your previous conversations or research to demonstrate a genuine understanding of their business challenges and goals.

4. Provide Value Upfront:

Start the conversation by offering immediate value. Share insights, industry trends, or relevant information that can benefit the prospect. By demonstrating your expertise and commitment to their success, you build trust from the outset.

5. Establish Common Ground:

Find common ground beyond business. Whether it's a shared hobby, a similar background, or a common goal, establishing a personal connection can create a more comfortable and open dialogue.

6. Be Transparent and Authentic:

Openness and authenticity are crucial in warm calling. Be transparent about your intentions and genuine in your interest. Authenticity builds trust and fosters a stronger connection with the prospect.

7. Create a Smooth Transition:

Seamlessly transition from the warm introduction to your business proposition. Clearly articulate how your product or service aligns with their needs and how the existing connection serves as a foundation for collaboration.

8. Acknowledge and Appreciate:

Express gratitude for the existing relationship or connection. Let the prospect know that you value their time and appreciate the opportunity to discuss potential collaboration. This reinforces a positive tone.

9. Be Flexible and Responsive:

Adapt your approach based on the prospect's response. Be flexible in tailoring your pitch to their evolving needs and concerns. A responsive and adaptive communication style enhances the warmth of the interaction.

10. Maintain Consistent Follow-Up:

Building a warm connection is an ongoing process. Regularly follow up with the prospect, sharing relevant updates, articles, or insights. Consistency reinforces your commitment and keeps the relationship alive.

By incorporating these warm calling strategies into your outreach, you can transform initial connections into meaningful, long-term relationships. Remember, the key is to build trust and demonstrate the value you bring to the prospect's business journey.

A typical sales funnel has stages like:

1. Awareness:

Introduce your product/service.

2. Interest:

Capture interest and provide more information.

3. Consideration:

Prospective customers evaluate the offering.

4. Intent:

The customer expresses the intent to purchase.

5. Purchase:

The customer completes the transaction.

6. Retention:

Efforts to keep customers engaged and satisfied.

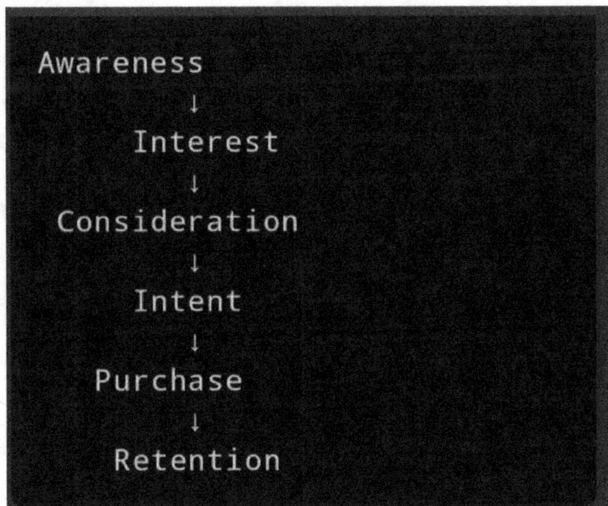

Fig.2: A Comprehensive Sales funnel

LESSON 11: MASTERING OBJECTION HANDLING

In the world of sales, objections are inevitable hurdles that can either hinder progress or become stepping stones to success. A skilled salesperson understands that objections are not roadblocks but rather opportunities to showcase value and address concerns. Let's explore ten common objections and effective strategies to overcome them.

Price Objection:

Objection: "Your product is too expensive."

- *Response:* Highlight the value proposition, emphasizing the long-term benefits and cost savings. Offer flexible payment plans or exclusive discounts for a limited period.

Timing Objection:

Objection: "Now is not the right time."

- *Response:* Showcase the urgency and immediate benefits of your product. Share success stories to illustrate the positive impact on those who acted promptly.

Authority Objection:

Objection: "I need to consult with my superior."

- *Response:* Provide informative materials tailored for decision-makers. Offer to set up a meeting with both parties to address any concerns directly.

Competition Objection:

Objection: "I'm considering other options."

- *Response:* Highlight key differentiators and success stories. Offer a competitive analysis, showcasing why your product surpasses alternatives.

Trust Objection:

Objection: "I'm not sure I can trust your company."

- *Response:* Share client testimonials, case studies, and industry awards to build credibility. Offer a trial period or a money-back guarantee to instill confidence.

Product Fit Objection:

Objection: "I'm not sure if your product fits our needs."

- *Response:* Conduct a thorough needs analysis to understand specific requirements. Showcase how your product addresses their pain points with real-life examples.

Risk Objection:

Objection: "I'm afraid of potential risks or complications."

- *Response:* Clearly outline your product's reliability and security measures. Offer a pilot program or a phased implementation to mitigate perceived risks.

Lack of Budget Objection:

Objection: "We don't have the budget for this."

- *Response:* Break down the cost over time or propose a scalable solution. Showcase the return on investment (ROI) and potential cost savings in the long run.

Perceived Complexity Objection:

Objection: "It seems too complicated for our team."

- *Response:* Offer training sessions and ongoing support. Provide user-friendly demonstrations and simplify complex features with real-world applications.

Previous Negative Experience Objection:

Objection: "We've had a bad experience with a similar product/service."

- *Response:* Acknowledge their concerns and share testimonials of clients who initially had reservations but found success with your solution. Highlight improvements and showcase your commitment to customer satisfaction.

Mastering objection handling is an essential skill in the sales landscape. By understanding these common objections and implementing strategic responses, you can turn challenges into opportunities and build stronger relationships with potential clients.

LESSON 12: MASTERING THE ART OF TONALITY

In sales,every word spoken holds the potential to sway a prospect's decision, tonality emerges as a formidable tool. The significance of tonality transcends mere communication; it becomes the melody that orchestrates successful sales conversations.

The Symphony of Persuasion

Tonality is the conductor of the sales symphony, setting the mood, tempo, and rhythm. A well-modulated voice can transform a mundane pitch into a captivating narrative. The subtle nuances of pitch, pace, and intonation wield immense influence, evoking emotions and creating a connection that transcends the transactional nature of the conversation.

Establishing Rapport

In the orchestra of sales, tonality is the bridge to establishing rapport. A warm and friendly tone invites the prospect into a conversation, creating a comfortable space where trust can flourish. Conversely, a harsh or monotone delivery may alienate potential clients, closing the door to meaningful engagement.

Conveying Confidence and Authority

A sales professional's tonality is a direct reflection of their confidence and authority. A firm and assured tone instills trust in the prospect, assuring them that the product or service being offered is not only valuable but also backed by a credible source. Conversely, a shaky or uncertain tone may cast doubt on the offering itself.

Emphasizing Key Points

Tonality serves as the highlighter of sales conversations, accentuating key points and crucial information. By employing variations in pitch and emphasis, a salesperson can guide the prospect's attention to the most vital aspects of the pitch, ensuring that the message is not only heard but also absorbed.

Navigating Objections with Grace

Encountering objections is an inevitable part of sales, and tonality becomes the armor that shields against resistance. A calm and empathetic tone can diffuse tension, turning objections into opportunities for further exploration. Conversely, a defensive or confrontational tone may escalate the situation, hindering the sales process.

Continuous Refinement

Just as a musician hones their craft through continuous practice, sales professionals must refine their tonal skills. Regular self-assessment, feedback from peers, and targeted training can contribute to the mastery of tonality, enabling salespeople to adapt their approach to diverse audiences and situations.

In conclusion, tonality in sales is not merely an afterthought but a strategic imperative. It is the melody that resonates with prospects, creating harmony in the sales journey. By understanding and harnessing the power of tonality, sales professionals can elevate their performance, orchestrate successful deals, and leave a lasting impression on every prospect they encounter.

LESSON 13: THE ART AND SCIENCE OF SALES

Fact 1: The Power of the First Impression

Did you know that it takes only seven seconds to make a first impression? In sales, those initial moments can make or break a deal. Ensure your handshake is firm, your smile is genuine, and your pitch is compelling to captivate your prospect from the start.

Fact 2: The Rule of 80/20

Ever heard of the Pareto Principle? In sales, approximately 80% of your revenue often comes from 20% of your customers. Focus on nurturing and retaining those high-value clients to maximize your sales success.

Fact 3: Timing is Everything

Studies show that Wednesdays and Thursdays are the best days for cold calling. Additionally, calling prospects between 4 pm and 5 pm can increase your chances of a successful conversation. Time your sales outreach strategically for optimal results.

Fact 4: The Follow-Up Dance

Around 80% of sales require at least five follow-ups after the initial contact. Persistence pays off in the world of sales, so don't be afraid to check in regularly without becoming overly pushy.

Fact 5: Storytelling Sells

People remember stories 22 times more than facts alone. Craft compelling narratives that resonate with your audience to make your sales pitches more memorable and emotionally engaging.

Fact 6: The Fear of Rejection

Did you know that, on average, it takes eight cold call attempts to reach a prospect? Embrace rejection as a stepping stone to success, learning from each experience to refine your approach and increase your conversion rates.

Fact 7: Social Selling Stats

Social media plays a crucial role in modern sales. Salespeople who use social selling are 50% more likely to meet or exceed their quotas. Leverage platforms like LinkedIn to build relationships, share insights, and expand your network.

Fact 8: Price Perception

Surprisingly, 60% of customers believe they are receiving a fair price if they understand the value of a product or service. Focus on effectively communicating the benefits to justify the cost and reinforce the value proposition.

Fact 9: Decision-Making in Seconds

Humans make decisions emotionally and then justify them logically. Tailor your sales approach to appeal to both aspects, addressing both the emotional desires and logical needs of your prospects.

Fact 10: Sales and Psychology

Utilize psychological triggers in your sales strategy. For example, offering limited-time discounts or emphasizing scarcity can create a sense of urgency, prompting quicker decision-making from potential customers. Understanding human psychology is a powerful tool in the sales arsenal.

LESSON 14: MASTERING THE ART OF CLOSING THE SALE

Closing the sale is a crucial step in the sales process, signaling the transition from building rapport to sealing the deal. Knowing when to close requires a keen understanding of your prospect's cues and the context of the conversation.

Here are some key indicators and examples to guide you through this pivotal stage:

Positive Buying Signals:

  - Example: If your prospect expresses enthusiasm, asks specific questions about the product or service, or nods in agreement, these positive signals indicate a readiness to move forward.

Identifying Decision-Making Moments:

  - Example: When your prospect starts discussing budget, timeline, or logistics, it's a sign that they are seriously considering the purchase. Use this opportunity to smoothly guide them toward the close.

Addressing Concerns:

  - Example: If your prospect raises objections, address them confidently. Once you've resolved their concerns, ask if they are ready to proceed, signaling a natural moment to close the sale.

Trial Closes:

- Example: Throughout the conversation, subtly introduce trial closes to gauge your prospect's readiness. For instance, you might say, "If we can meet your specific requirements, would you be comfortable moving forward?"

Time Sensitivity:

- Example: If your product or service has a limited-time offer or promotion, use it strategically to create a sense of urgency. This can prompt the prospect to make a decision sooner rather than later.

Assessing Engagement Level:

- Example: Pay attention to the prospect's body language and verbal cues. If they are leaning in, making eye contact, and showing genuine interest, it might be the ideal moment to propose the close.

Confirmation of Benefits:

- Example: Summarize the key benefits and value propositions your product or service offers. Ask the prospect if these align with their needs and if they see the value in moving forward.

Asking Directly:

- Example: Sometimes, a straightforward approach works best. You can ask directly, "Based on our discussion today, are you ready to proceed with the purchase?"

Remember, closing is not about pressuring the prospect but

guiding them to a decision that aligns with their needs. Adapt your approach based on the individual and the specific context of the sales conversation. Mastering the art of closing takes practice, so refine your skills through experience and learn from each interaction to continually improve your sales techniques.

LESSON 15: MASTERING CLOSING TECHNIQUES

In the art of sales, the closing phase is where the magic happens. It's the culmination of your efforts to build rapport, present value, and address objections. Here are some powerful closing techniques to seal the deal:

1. The Assumptive Close:

- Assume the sale is already complete. For example, "When would be the best time for our team to start implementing the solution?"

2. The Alternative Close:

- Present two options, both leading to a positive outcome. This empowers the prospect by giving them a sense of control. "Would you prefer delivery in two weeks or a month?"

3. The Ben Franklin Close:

- Encourage the prospect to list pros and cons. Then, guide them to the conclusion that your product or service outweighs any potential drawbacks.

4. The Now or Never Close:

- Create a sense of urgency. "This special offer is valid only until the end of the week. Can I count on you to make a decision by then?"

5. The Puppy Dog Close:

- Offer a trial or a limited experience so the prospect can "try before they buy." Once they've experienced the benefits, it's harder to say no.

6. The Takeaway Close:

- Briefly withdraw an offer to make the prospect realize its value. "I understand if this isn't the right fit for you. Shall I go ahead and cancel the order?"

7. The Summary Close:

- Recap the key benefits and features, emphasizing how your solution addresses their specific needs. "So, with our product, you not only save time but also reduce costs and increase efficiency. Can we move forward?"

8. The Porcupine Close:

- Respond to objections with questions that lead the prospect to their own resolution. "I see your concern about the price. What would the impact be on your team's productivity if you had a tool that could streamline their workflow?"

Remember, the key to successful closing is to be adaptable. Pay attention to the prospect's cues and tailor your approach accordingly. Building trust and understanding their needs will ultimately guide you to the most effective closing technique for each unique situation.

Script template

Below is a template and an example of a script you could use. Amend and adapt to the needs of your client,product or industry.

1. Opening Statements:

- "Hello, [Prospect's Name], this is [Your Name] from [Your Company]."

- "Thank you for taking my call today."

- "I hope I'm not catching you at a bad time."

2. Building Rapport:

- "How's your day going so far?"

- "I noticed [something relevant about the prospect's company]."

3. Qualifying Questions:

- "Can you tell me more about your current challenges in [specific area]?"

- "What goals are you looking to achieve in the next [timeframe]?"

4. Features and Benefits:

- "Our product/service can help you by [highlighting a key benefit]."

- "One unique aspect of our offering is [mention a standout feature]."

5. Overcoming Objections:

- "I understand your concern; many of our clients initially felt the same way. However, what they found was [share a success story or case study]."

- "Let me address that by explaining how [feature] directly addresses your concern."

6. Closing the Sale:

- "Based on our conversation, it seems like [product/service] aligns well with your needs. Would you like to move forward?"

- "I recommend our [specific package] as it includes [highlight additional value]."

7. Handling Rejections:

- "I appreciate your honesty. Can you share what aspect isn't resonating with you, so I can better understand your perspective?"

- "If there's a specific concern, I'm here to address it. Is there anything I can clarify or modify to make this a better fit for you?"

8. Follow-up:

- "Would it be helpful if I checked in with you [specific time] to see how things are progressing?"

- "I'll send you an email with more information. Feel free to reach out if you have any questions."

9. Closing Courtesies:

- "Thank you for your time and consideration today."

- "I look forward to the possibility of working together."

10. Continuous Improvement:

- "What feedback do you have for me regarding our conversation?"

- "Is there anything I could have done differently to better meet your needs?"

LESSON 16: NINE MORE EFFECTIVE SALES CLOSING TECHNIQUES

1. The Trial Close:

- Encourage a small commitment or agreement before finalizing the sale. "Would you like to proceed with the standard package, or are you leaning towards the premium option?"

2. The Fear of Loss Close:

- Highlight what the prospect stands to lose by not making a decision now. "Given the high demand for this product, delaying your decision might mean missing out on the current promotional pricing."

3. The Question Close:

- Prompt the prospect to answer in a way that naturally leads to a positive decision. "Based on what we've discussed, do you see how our solution can address your specific challenges?"

4. The Referral Close:

- Mention successful client experiences to instill confidence. "Many clients who faced similar issues found our product to be a game-changer. Would you like me to connect you with one of them for a quick chat?"

5. The Budget Close:

- If cost is a concern, break it down into smaller, manageable amounts. "Considering the long-term benefits, the monthly cost for our service is actually equivalent to a cup of coffee per day. Does that align with your budget?"

6. The Summary of Benefits Close:

- Reiterate the key benefits and advantages of your product or service. "Just to recap, our solution not only saves you time but also enhances your team's productivity. Are you ready to move forward?"

7. The Take-It-Away Close:

- Create a sense of scarcity by temporarily removing an option. "I can only reserve this special discount for you until the end of today. Shall I go ahead and finalize the order?"

8. The Urgency Close:

- Emphasize a time-sensitive element to prompt a quicker decision. "Our current inventory is limited, and the next shipment isn't due for another month. Would you like to secure your order before stocks run out?"

9. The Socratic Close:

- Use open-ended questions to guide the prospect towards realizing the value of your offering. "How do you envision our product making a positive impact on your operations?"

Remember, the effectiveness of these techniques depends on your understanding of the prospect's needs and the ability to tailor your approach accordingly. Adaptability and active listening play crucial roles in mastering the art of sales closing.

LESSON 17: MASTERING ELOCUTION

The art of elocution holds a paramount role in influencing potential clients and closing deals. Elocution is not merely about speaking clearly; it's a nuanced skill that combines tone, pitch, pace, and articulation to convey confidence, credibility, and conviction. Here, we delve into the crucial aspects of elocution and how they can be harnessed to boost your sales prowess.

Clarity is Key

Elocution in sales begins with clarity. Ensure your words are well-articulated and easy to comprehend. Speak with precision, avoiding jargon that might confuse your audience. A clear message instills confidence and trust in your clients.

Mastering Tone and Pitch

The tone of your voice sets the emotional tone of the conversation. Adjust it to match the mood of your message – be it excitement, reassurance, or empathy. Similarly, pitch variation adds dynamism to your speech, preventing monotony and maintaining your listener's engagement.

The Power of Pace

Controlled pacing is a secret weapon in elocution for sales. Adjust your speed to emphasize key points, slowing down for emphasis and speeding up to build excitement. This keeps your audience attentive and responsive.

Harnessing Silence

Elocution isn't just about what you say but also about when you choose to say it. Embrace strategic pauses to let your words sink in and give your audience time to process information. Silence can be a powerful tool in creating suspense and anticipation.

Confidence in Conviction

Believe in what you're saying, and let that belief shine through in your voice. Confidence in your message is contagious and instills faith in your clients. Work on eliminating any verbal hesitations to project unwavering assurance.

Adaptability is a Virtue

Understanding your audience is paramount. Adjust your elocution style based on who you're speaking to – whether it's a corporate executive or a small business owner. Adapting your approach fosters better communication and connection.

Storytelling for Impact

Elocution is not just a series of statements; it's an opportunity to weave a compelling narrative. Craft stories that resonate with your clients, making your pitch memorable and emotionally impactful. A well-told story can leave a lasting impression.

Feedback as a Refinement Tool

Regularly seek feedback on your elocution from colleagues or mentors. Constructive criticism helps refine your delivery, identifying areas for improvement and reinforcing your strengths.

Mastering elocution in sales is an ongoing journey. It's a blend of art and science, where the right combination of words, tone, and delivery can turn a casual conversation into a compelling sales pitch. Invest time in honing your elocution skills, and witness the transformative impact on your sales success.

LESSON 18: MASTERING NLP

In the dynamic world of sales, effective communication is the cornerstone of success. Neuro-Linguistic Programming (NLP) offers powerful techniques to enhance your sales conversations, build rapport, and close deals.

Let's explore some key strategies to leverage NLP in the sales process.

Establish Rapport:

Building a strong connection with your prospect is crucial. Mirroring and matching their body language, tone, and language patterns create a subconscious bond. Pay attention to their preferred sensory modality – whether they are visual, auditory, or kinesthetic – and tailor your communication accordingly.

Use Anchoring Techniques:

Create positive associations by anchoring specific gestures, words, or tones with positive emotions. When strategically deployed during your sales pitch, these anchors can trigger positive responses and influence decision-making.

Utilize Embedded Commands:

Incorporate subtle commands within your language to guide your prospect's thoughts. Phrases like "Imagine how this solution can benefit your team" or "Consider the possibilities" plant seeds that encourage the prospect to envision a positive outcome.

Storytelling with Sensory Language:

Craft compelling narratives using sensory-rich language. Appeal to your prospect's emotions by describing scenarios that evoke vivid mental images. This helps create a memorable and persuasive narrative that resonates with their needs and desires.

Pace and Lead:

Adapt your communication style to match the prospect's pace, then gradually introduce subtle changes to guide the conversation. This technique ensures a smooth transition and enhances receptivity to your suggestions.

Listen Actively:

Effective communication is a two-way street. Practice active listening to understand your prospect's concerns, desires, and motivations. Use their own words in your responses to establish rapport and demonstrate empathy.

Frame Your Proposition Positively:

Present your product or service in a way that emphasizes benefits over features. Use positive language to highlight how your solution addresses the prospect's challenges and contributes to their success.

Overcome Objections with Reframing:

When faced with objections, reframe them as opportunities. NLP techniques allow you to guide the prospect's perspective, turning challenges into solutions and emphasizing the positive aspects of your offering.

Mastering Eye Accessing Cues:

Observe your prospect's eye movements to gain insights into their thought processes. While not foolproof, these cues can provide valuable information about whether they are accessing visual, auditory, or kinesthetic information – allowing you to tailor your communication accordingly.

Build Confidence with Future Pacing:

Guide the prospect's imagination towards a positive future scenario after choosing your product or service. This instills confidence and helps them visualize the positive outcomes they can achieve by making the desired decision.

Incorporating these NLP techniques into your sales approach can significantly enhance your ability to connect with prospects, understand their needs, and ultimately close deals successfully. As with any skill, consistent practice and refinement will contribute to your mastery of NLP in the sales domain.

LESSON 19: NAVIGATING BUYER'S REMORSE AND BUILDING CUSTOMER LOYALTY

Buyer's remorse is a common phenomenon that businesses encounter, but it doesn't have to be the end of the customer journey. In fact, it can be an opportunity to strengthen the relationship with your customers. Here's a guide on how to handle buyer's remorse and retain customers effectively.

Understanding buyers remorse

Empathy is Key:

Begin by acknowledging the customer's feelings. Show empathy and understanding towards their concerns. This helps in building trust and opening lines of communication.

Timely Response:

Address buyer's remorse promptly. The sooner you engage with the customer, the more likely you are to alleviate their concerns. Timely responses demonstrate your commitment to customer satisfaction.

Strategies to Overcome Buyer's Remorse

Educate and Communicate:

Provide additional information about the product or service. Sometimes, remorse stems from a lack of understanding or unrealistic expectations. Educate customers on the benefits and usage to reaffirm their decision.

Offer Solutions:

Identify specific concerns and propose solutions. This could involve refunds, exchanges, or additional support. Tailor your approach to the individual situation, showing a willingness to make things right.

Building Customer Loyalty

Personalized Follow-Up:

After resolving the immediate issue, follow up with a personalized message. Express your gratitude for their business and inquire about their overall experience. This human touch can make a significant impact.

Exclusive Offers and Discounts:

Provide exclusive offers or discounts as a gesture of goodwill. This not only compensates for any inconvenience but also encourages the customer to continue their relationship with your business.

Long-Term Customer Retention Strategies

Quality Customer Service:

Consistently deliver exceptional customer service. A positive experience in addressing buyer's remorse creates a lasting impression, making customers more likely to return.

Feedback Loop:

Establish a feedback loop where customers can share their experiences. Use this valuable input to continually improve your products and services, demonstrating a commitment to meeting customer needs.

Cultivating a Positive Reputation

Transparency and Honesty:

Be transparent about your products or services. Honest communication builds trust, reducing the likelihood of buyer's remorse in the first place.

Community Engagement:

Foster a sense of community around your brand. Engage

customers through social media and other platforms, creating a space where they feel connected to your business and each other.

By proactively addressing buyer's remorse and implementing customer retention strategies, businesses can not only salvage a potentially negative situation but also create loyal customers who contribute to long-term success. Remember, every interaction is an opportunity to build a lasting relationship with your customers.

LESSON 20: WISDOM FROM JIM ROHN

In the realm of personal development and success, few voices resonate as powerfully as that of Jim Rohn. His insights and timeless wisdom continue to inspire and guide individuals on their journey towards a fulfilling life. Let's explore a chapter enriched with 10 profound quotes from the legendary Jim Rohn.

1. "You are the average of the five people you spend the most time with."

Surround yourself with those who uplift and challenge you, for they shape your reality.

2. "Don't wish it was easier, wish you were better."

Embrace challenges as opportunities for growth, for therein lies the path to improvement.

3. "Discipline is the bridge between goals and accomplishment."

Consistent effort and self-discipline pave the way to turning aspirations into reality.

4. "Take care of your body. It's the only place you have to live."

Prioritize your health, for it is the foundation upon which all other achievements are built.

5. "Success is neither magical nor mysterious. Success is the natural consequence of consistently applying the basic fundamentals."

Establish strong habits and stay committed to the fundamentals of your craft.

6. "If you are not willing to risk the usual, you will have to settle for the ordinary."

Boldness and a willingness to step outside your comfort zone distinguish the extraordinary from the ordinary.

7. "Don't join an easy crowd; you won't grow. Go where the expectations and the demands to perform are high."

Challenge yourself by seeking environments that foster growth and demand excellence.

8. "Don't let your learning lead to knowledge. Let your learning lead to action."

Apply what you learn, for it is in the execution that knowledge transforms into power.

9. "Motivation is what gets you started. Habit is what keeps you going."

Cultivate positive habits that propel you forward, as they are the key to sustained success.

10. "The major value in life is not what you get. The major value in life is what you become."

Focus on personal development and character, as they define the true measure of a successful life.

LESSON 21: MASTERING THE ART OF WORK-LIFE BALANCE

Achieving success goes beyond closing deals—it involves crafting a lifestyle that sustains both personal and professional growth. A successful salesman understands the delicate balance between ambition and well-being.

Morning Rituals:

The day begins early for the accomplished sales professional. Establishing a consistent morning routine helps set a positive tone. This might include exercise, meditation, and a healthy breakfast to fuel the day ahead.

Continuous Learning:

Success is synonymous with growth. Top salesmen dedicate time each day to staying informed about industry trends, product knowledge, and refining their sales techniques. Embracing a mindset of continuous learning is pivotal.

Time Management:

Effective time management distinguishes the best salespeople. Prioritizing tasks, setting goals, and utilizing productivity tools enable them to stay organized and focused, ensuring that every minute contributes to their success.

Networking Mastery:

Beyond the office walls, successful salespeople engage in strategic networking. They attend industry events, participate in conferences, and cultivate meaningful relationships with clients and colleagues. Networking isn't just a task—it's a lifestyle.

Adaptability:

Flexibility is key in the ever-evolving sales landscape. Successful salesmen embrace change and continuously adapt to new technologies, market dynamics, and customer preferences. This adaptability ensures they remain ahead of the curve.

Mental Resilience:

Sales is a profession filled with highs and lows. A resilient mindset is crucial for handling rejection, navigating challenging situations, and maintaining composure during negotiations. Successful salesmen view setbacks as opportunities to learn and improve.

Work-Life Harmony:

Striking a balance between professional and personal life is fundamental. Successful salespeople recognize the importance of quality time with family and friends, as well as pursuing hobbies and interests outside of work. This harmony enhances overall well-being.

Effective Communication:

Clear and persuasive communication is at the core of successful salesmanship. Beyond business transactions, the ability to connect on a personal level fosters trust and loyalty, leading to long-term success.

Goal Setting:

Setting ambitious yet achievable goals propels successful salesmen forward. These goals act as a roadmap, providing direction and motivation to reach new heights in their career.

Giving Back:

A sense of purpose extends beyond the boardroom. Many successful sales professionals engage in philanthropy and community service, contributing to causes that align with their values. This not only makes a positive impact but also enhances personal fulfillment.

In essence, the lifestyle of a successful salesman encompasses a holistic approach to personal and professional development. It is a continuous journey of self-improvement, adaptability, and a commitment to maintaining a harmonious balance between the demands of the career and the joys of life.

LESSON 22: THE IMPACT OF ARTIFICIAL INTELLIGENCE ON SALES

In the fast-evolving landscape of sales, Artificial Intelligence (AI) has emerged as a powerful force, transforming traditional approaches and ushering in a new era of efficiency and effectiveness. However, like any technological advancement, AI in sales comes with its own set of pros and cons, shaping the way businesses engage with customers and drive revenue.

Pros

1. Data-Driven Insights:

AI empowers sales teams with unparalleled access to data, allowing for a deeper understanding of customer behavior and preferences. Through advanced analytics, businesses can make informed decisions, optimizing their strategies to align with market trends and individual customer needs.

2. Personalization:

AI enables personalized customer experiences by analyzing vast datasets to predict customer preferences. This personal touch in sales interactions can significantly enhance customer satisfaction and loyalty, ultimately driving higher conversion rates.

3. Efficient Lead Generation:

With AI-driven tools, sales teams can automate and streamline lead generation processes. Predictive analytics and machine learning algorithms help identify high-potential leads, saving time and resources that can be redirected towards cultivating meaningful relationships.

4. Chatbots and Virtual Assistants:

AI-powered chatbots provide instant responses to customer queries, ensuring round-the-clock engagement. Virtual assistants not only enhance customer service but also aid sales representatives by automating routine tasks, freeing up their time for more strategic activities.

5. Sales Forecasting Accuracy:

AI algorithms analyze historical data and market trends, contributing to more accurate sales forecasting. This allows businesses to make well-informed decisions about inventory, staffing, and overall resource allocation.

Cons

1. Job Displacement:

The integration of AI in sales processes may lead to concerns about job displacement, particularly for routine and repetitive tasks. Sales roles relying heavily on manual processes may be at risk as automation becomes more prevalent.

2. Over-Reliance on Technology:

While AI is a valuable tool, over-reliance on technology can lead to a disconnect between sales professionals and their customers. Genuine human connection is crucial in building trust, and an excessive dependence on AI may hinder the development of these relationships.

3. Privacy and Security Concerns:

The vast amounts of customer data processed by AI systems raise concerns about privacy and security. Businesses must navigate the delicate balance of leveraging customer information for personalized experiences without compromising data integrity.

4. Initial Implementation Costs:

Adopting AI in sales requires a significant upfront investment in technology, training, and infrastructure. Small and medium-sized businesses may face challenges in absorbing these costs, potentially creating a barrier to entry for some.

5. Ethical Considerations:

The use of AI in sales raises ethical questions, especially when it comes to data usage and decision-making. Businesses must be transparent in their AI practices and ensure ethical guidelines are in place to prevent unintended consequences.

In conclusion, the integration of AI into sales processes presents a dynamic landscape with both promise and challenges. Striking the right balance between leveraging the advantages of AI while addressing its limitations is crucial for businesses aiming to stay competitive in an ever-evolving market.

LESSON 23: BEYOND THE SALE - A JOURNEY OF GROWTH AND SUCCESS

As we conclude this exploration into the world of sales, remember that the journey doesn't end with the closing of a deal. Instead, it extends into a realm of continuous growth, personal development, and enduring success. In this final chapter, let's reflect on the key takeaways and set the stage for what lies beyond the pages of this book.

Eternal Student of Salesmanship:

Sales is a dynamic field, constantly evolving with market trends and consumer behaviors. Commit yourself to being an eternal student of salesmanship, embracing new strategies, technologies, and insights that shape the ever-changing landscape.

Cultivating Relationships:

Beyond transactions, true success in sales is built on authentic and lasting relationships. Nurture connections with clients, colleagues, and industry professionals. Your network is not just a resource; it's a community that supports your journey.

Adapting to Change:

The business world is characterized by flux, and adaptability is the key to survival. Embrace change with a positive mindset, viewing challenges as opportunities for innovation and growth. Your ability to adapt will distinguish you in the competitive realm of sales.

Ethics and Integrity:

Uphold the highest standards of ethics and integrity in every interaction. Trust is the foundation of successful sales relationships, and maintaining your reputation as a trustworthy professional will contribute to your long-term success.

Balancing Ambition and Well-being:

As you strive for professional excellence, don't lose sight of your personal well-being. Success is not solely measured by revenue but also by a balanced and fulfilling life. Remember to celebrate achievements, practice self-care, and maintain a healthy work-life balance.

Paying It Forward:

The knowledge and skills gained on your sales journey are valuable resources. Consider mentoring aspiring professionals, sharing your experiences, and contributing to the growth of others within the sales community. Paying it forward creates a legacy of success.

Continued Learning:

The sales landscape will continue to evolve, presenting new challenges and opportunities. Stay curious, engage in ongoing learning, and seek out insights from various sources. A commitment to continuous improvement ensures your relevance and adaptability.

As you close the final chapter of this book, remember that your journey in sales is a story that unfolds with each client interaction, every negotiation, and all the lessons learned along the way. Your path to success is uniquely yours, and the possibilities are boundless.

Thank you for embarking on this journey of salesmanship with me. May your future endeavors be filled with meaningful connections, unprecedented achievements, and the unwavering determination to shape a legacy of success in the dynamic world of sales.

Here's to your continued growth, prosperity, and the endless possibilities that await you in the chapters yet to be written.

Best wishes on your sales journey!

Sincerely,

Chris Edun